Also by J. R. Solonche from Deerbrook Editions

I, Emily Dickinson & Other Found Poems
Won't Be Long
Beautiful Day

For Amanda!

Tomorrow,

Today,

And Yesterday

poems

J.R. Solonche

DEERBROOK EDITIONS

PUBLISHED BY
Deerbrook Editions
P.O. Box 542
Cumberland, ME 04021
www.deerbrookeditions.com
www.issuu.com/deerbrookeditions

FIRST EDITION
© 2019 by J. R. Solonche
All rights reserved
ISBN: 978-0-9991062-9-7

Book design by Jeffrey Haste

Contents

My Haiku	11
Caliban	12
Short Speech For Sisyphus	13
After The Movie	14
First Peony	15
The Sunlight	16
October	17
Toy Poem	18
The Dead Are So Spiteful	19
When Emily	20
Virginia Creeper	21
Question For Yahweh	22
In The Car	23
Someday The Last Poet In The World	24
Sonnet Of The Poem Genome	25
The Title Of My Only Novel	26
The First Two Sentences Of My Only Novel	27
The Last Sentence Of My Only Novel	28
Byron	39
Poison Ivy	30
Emergencies	31
A Walk	32
Ode To The East Wind	33
If Trees Could Weep	34
Sort Of Sonnet	35
Looking Out The Window While Listening To The World Series	36
Timeline	37
Sitting On A Bench	38
Trees Leaning On Lines	39
Impatience	40
Willow	41
Delphinium	42
Sunflower For Maggie By Georgia O'Keeffe	43
Full Moon	44
Now That	45

Idol Worship	46
Improvisation	47
Recreation	48
Another Walk	49
Gerald Stern	50
Poetry Month At Storm King	51
The River	52
Poetry	53
Recital	54
Echo And Narcissus	55
Milton	56
The Moon Over The Hill In The Middle Of The Day	57
Country Cemetery Under Three Feet Of Snow	58
Detour	59
How Beautifully The Lilacs Lie	60
The Skylight Of The Westchester Mall	61
Poem Using A Line From A Poem By Alberto Rios	62
In The Waiting Room Waiting My Turn	63
Pythagoras Was The First Philosopher To Call Himself That	64
Soon It Will Be Spring	65
Uncollecting	66
Emily At Two: A Photograph	67
Swans	68
March	69
A Pair Of Boxer Shorts Given Me As A Birthday Gift	70
Today Spring Leaves My Mind And Enters A Cloud	71
I Am Looking Forward To Cremation	72
Woodstock	73
His Life At Home	74
The Most Dangerous People	75
Fallen Barn	76
Paterson	77
Daffodils	78
Projection	79
To A Student Who May Not Pass Writing	80
Wedding	81

A Stone	82
New York Movie By Edward Hopper	83
The Golden Rule According To Emily	84
Reassurance	85
Bad Day At The Piano	86
Claim to Fame	87
Present	88
Dialogue	89
The Rain	90
In Four Months	91
If It Weren't For	92
In The Middle Of The Lake	93
In Yosemite	94
The Jonah Story	95
My Friend Jim Says	96
I'm In Love With The Starbucks Mermaid	97
Building Site	98
Classroom	99
Eden	100
Ten Dollars	101
Myopia	102
Forgetting The Book	103
Apology To Mary Adoki	104
Orange Buds By Mail From Florida By Walt Whitman	105
Typo	106
October Rain	107
The Dark Rabbi And The Rose Rabbi	108
Dunkin Donuts	109
Wake	110
Him To The Sun	112
Utility	113
A Brief Conversation	114
The End	115
Tomorrow, Today, And Yesterday	116
Acknowledgements	119

Tomorrow,
Today,
and Yesterday

My Haiku

J. R. Solonche (Hey!)
Post Office Box Ninety-nine.
Blooming Grove, New York.

Caliban

They are gone, all gone.
And Ariel, too. Good riddance.

The place is mine, all mine!
Oh shit . . . there's no one left to curse.

Short Speech For Sisyphus

See how I torment
my tormentor

by cutting
him out.

See how I punish
myself by pushing this

stone I cut
up this mountain I built.

After The Movie

"See? It didn't end so badly,"
I said.

"She didn't die.
She only got married off

to that old man."
You didn't say anything.

But the look you gave me
was so deeply cutting,

it severed my balls
from the inside.

First Peony

Big, brassy, over-rouged,
it sashays on its stalk in the breeze.

It will have the place to itself for a week,
street walker who has found a new street before her sisters.

The Sunlight

becomes the windows
of the Holy Cross

Monastery in many colors,
but not one, not one, not one remains

the untransubstantiated
light of truth.

October

The red headed woodpecker
knocked on the door of the oak
so persistently until the old crow
three trees over finally spoke,
Go, go, go, go, go.

Toy Poem

This is my toy poem.
I hope you like it.
I made it in the workshop.

I sawed it and sanded it
and glued it and screwed
it and painted it and

finished it to a glossy
finish and signed my
name on the bottom of it.

Please don't pick it up.
Please don't play with it.
It will fall apart.

The Dead Are So Spiteful

The dead are so cruel.
So hard.

So spiteful.
They want to take

all our words away
with them

to their silent place.
They want

to leave us with nothing
but their names.

Yes,
the dead are so spiteful.

When Emily

came into the house
and the door
didn't close completely
behind her,
she called out, "Dad,
could you close
the rest of the door?"

Virginia Creeper

It wouldn't surprise me
if it crept all the way
up from Virginia.

Witness these crossing
the road as if on a dare
from the ferns on the other side.

Question For Yahweh

If, as is said,
you are omnipotent,

and since, as is said,
omnipotence means

for you all things are possible,
why the hell are you always so old?

In The Car

A FOUND POEM

"My thoughts
aren't deep
enough for poems,"
she said.

Someday The Last Poet In The World

will write the world's last poem.
Someday the last reader in the world
will read it and say to herself,
"Where is Emily Dickinson when you need her?"

Sonnet Of The Poem Genome

Angel, blind bud, calm arrow,
cross curse. Delight dew bride
dream eagle, eternal brow.
Evil evening fate, faith child,

fountain flock fate fox crown.
Gentle, glad glory, grape beast,
grief guest hill. Hell dawn
ivory hawk image, lamb feast

joy. Life lion lord, meadow prayer
melody mercy noble perfume. Passion,
pity, pride, pool purple, shower
rapture, raven robe, rock rose vision.

Sorrow, sorrow soul spirit, storm veil,
wisdom, wandering, weeping sword-soul.

The Title Of My One And Only Novel

Just Fine

The First Two Sentences Of My One And Only Novel

Justin Fine was going to his first funeral.
He was 44 years old.

The Last Sentence Of My One And Only Novel

Everything, he told himself, was going to be just fine.

Byron

I did not shave today.
What for?
Where was I going?
What was I doing?
Was I going to Buckingham Palace?
Was I going to be knighted by the queen?
I know what Byron said.
I know he said that shaving
is man's punishment for eating of the fruit
of the Tree of Knowledge.
Of course, he could have stopped shaving.
He could have grown a beard.
He could have been Tennyson.
Maybe he would have.
If only he hadn't died in Greece.
If only that had been a close shave.

Poison Ivy

You poor child!
You poor tomato-faced child!

What bright crimson punishment,
what ten days in itching hell,

what metamorphosis,
all for touching the crown of the ivy god.

You poor child!
You poor fire-faced child!

Emergencies

In case of Jewish wedding, break glass.
In case of irreconcilable differences, break up.
In case of guests, break bread.
In case of beans, break wind.
In case of bull, break china.
In case of loss of faith, break vows.
In case of bribe, break word.
In case of breach, break through.
In case of musical, break leg.
In case of last straw, break camel's back.
In case of sidewalk crack, break devil's back.
In case of nonpayment, break knee caps.
In case of billiards, break clean.
In case of rouge, break bank.
In case of Knicks, break fast.
In case of birth, break water.
In case of Willie Sutton, break in.
In case of Alcatraz, break out.
In case of hives, break out.
In case of Jerry Lewis, break up.
In case of Martin and Lewis, break up.
In case of all hell, break loose.

A Walk

Between one rain and another rain,
I go for a walk around the campus block,

my big umbrella in my back pocket.
I cannot see what I look like,

but a student passing me, seeing what I look like,
turns her head a little back and grins.

Ode To The East Wind

Gnieb s'nmutuA fo htaerb uoht,
        dniW tseW dliw O

? dniheb raf eb gnirpS nac,
        semoc retniW fi

, dniw, O! ycehporp a fo
        tepmurt ehT

htrae denekawanu ot spil ym
        hguorht eB

If Trees Could Weep

If pine and oak, ash
and larch, sassafras
and sycamore, if all
of them could weep,
they should weep
like the weeping cherry
tree whose snow white
tears are more beautiful
than laughter.

Sort Of Sonnet

I
am
not

sure
about
poetry

however
composed,
necessary,

absolutely
spontaneous,
premeditated,

unpredictable,
underestimated.

Looking Out The Window While Listening To The World Series

The jet
winds up

and pitches
itself.

The wind
swings

and
misses.

The jet
disappears

into
the white

catcher's mitt
of cloud.

Timeline

1819......Walt Whitman is born.
1821......John Keats dies.
1883......William Carlos Williams is born.
1892......Walt Whitman dies.

Sitting On A Bench

in the park next to
a planting of flowers,
trying to think of nothing,
I sneezed. A stranger
passing at that moment
said, "Bless you."
"Thank you," I said.
I must have succeeded at
thinking of nothing, for
I really felt blessed,
and I really was thankful.

Trees Leaning On Lines

I had to call the power
company. I know there is
no dignity in the chainsaw
sawing through, none in
not going back to soil
whole, but I had to call.
I'm sure they weren't
observant. I'm sure
there was nowhere else
for them to fall.

Impatience

How impatient life is.
The ice is not yet gone from the lake,
and the carp are already awake with both eyes,
and yesterday, as I watched, the mourning doves mated.

Willow

Willow may be old,
but it hasn't forgotten
how to make green green.

Delphinium

Back from the brink
of drowning,

death from so much rain,
drenched,

yet it revives
under the golden hands

of the sun,
breathes again,

reborn blue
of purple birth,

colored to our
opposite expectation.

Sunflower For Maggie By Georgia O'Keeffe

She's picked it out
from the chorus line of van Gogh's vase

and given it its close-up:
Broad goofy grin of a flower,

mouth full of gold,
shrugging green shoulders at the world.

Full Moon

With hope as
bright as this,

we could dazzle
a world of despair.

With an edge
as keen as this,

we could sever
soul from body

and never
know it.

Now That

the cherry tree
in front
of the house
looks like
every other tree,
I will look
at every other
tree with my
cherry tree eyes.

Idol Worship

The judge's advice to the singer
was not to open his mouth,
or to open his throat,
or to open his chest,
or to open his heart.
The judge's advice to the singer
was, "Open your eyes."

Improvisation

When my wife
is out of sorts,

the solution
is at hand.

Recreation

We, too, are here
in summer,
at the seashore,
playing to make
ourselves again
for the workings
of another year.

Another Walk

"Extend yourself," you said
walking briskly on the road
four steps ahead of me,
while I, eyeing your behind,
was thinking how much
nicer it would be to extend myself in bed.

Gerald Stern

You see, it's all crazy, all crazy.
There is a tree, a sycamore.
And there is the Ohio.
There is the Oder.
They are one river.
There is slavery.
And there is the Holocaust.
They are one abomination.
They are like two rivers flowing one into the
other to make one river.
The Ohio and the Oder are one river.
It's all crazy, so crazy.
You see, we are all crazy like that sometimes.
You see, the world does that sometimes.
It makes us into its own crazy image.
You see, some more than others,
some more often than others,
some for longer than others.

Poetry Month At Storm King

Everything was fine
at Kay Ryan's
reading until
someone in
the toilet nearby,
the door very open,
flushed down
her last line.

The River

The mountains on the other side
of the river

do not talk to the mountains
on this side of the river,

but the river speaks to the mountains
on both sides with one voice.

Poetry

A student came to my office.
"I know what I want to say,
but I don't know how to say it,"
he said. "No problem," I said.
"Read through this for a while,"
I told him as I handed him
a fat anthology of contemporary
American poetry. "You'll learn
how to say it sooner or later."
Another student came to my office.
"I don't know what to say, but
I have this funny feeling that
I already know how to say it,"
he said. "No problem. You're
already a poet," I said as I waved
him out of my office and down,
down the long, long, dark, dark stairs.

Recital

In the center of the stage,
the piano, exactly in the center
waiting for the pianist to make love to it,
waiting for the audience,
who is talking to itself, to say, "Ah,
how beautifully the pianist plays the piano,"
when instead it should say,
"Ah, how beautifully they play the music."
Exactly where the music is,
the piano sings its silence,
its mouth wide open,
in one breath, as God did once,
but never again.

Echo And Narcissus

All of them loved him,
but he loved none of them.

So one must wonder
about his home life,

which cannot have been simple.
And was she so normal,

that Echo, that would-be wife
of such an ego, of such a narcissist?

Milton

Milton showed
that darkness
can be bright. Well,

he was blind,
which makes him right.
At least in hell.

The Moon Over The Hill In The Middle Of The Day

O, over-the-hill
movie star,

so that's what
you look like

without all
the face powder.

Country Cemetery Under Three Feet Of Snow

Only the tops of the two
tallest stones are visible.
The rest are buried totally,
as buried as the dead beneath
them. I do not linger here.
Instead, I will come back
in spring, when the snow
is gone, when all the stones
are open in the sun like gray
flowers among the daffodils.
When death really hits home.

Detour

How lost
we are off

the beaten path.
When we have

to go back,
how taken aback.

How Beautifully The Lilacs Lie

"We are the be all and end all," they sigh.
How beautifully the lilacs lie.

"We are the perfumed apples of your eye."
How beautifully the lilacs lie.

"We are your comfort when you die."
How beautifully the lilacs lie.

The Skylight Of The Westchester Mall

If everything that is precious
to us can only be found in glass cases,
then for whom are we precious
in this glass case we find ourselves?
And for whom is that perfect blue
and white heaven heaven?

Poem Using A Line From A Poem By Alberto Rios

"How true," you said when I showed it to you:
Words are our weakest hold on the world.
"How much stronger touch is. And smell.
And hearing. And sight, too, is a stronger hold
on the world than words. But your words,
you know, are your strongest hold on me."

That was a warning.

In The Waiting Room Waiting My Turn

In the waiting room waiting my turn
in the dentist's office, I am alternating
reading a fashion magazine
and looking out the window. Reading?
No, there's nothing to read in the fashion
magazine. Looking? So I am alternating
looking at the pictures of the fashionable
in this month's fashion magazine
and reading the venetian blinds horizontal
on the window, which teaches me a great deal
about the sky and the sky blue it has always been.

Pythagoras Was The First Philosopher To Call Himself That

So one must wonder what
the philosophers who did not

call themselves that then called themselves.
Thinkers? Wonderers? Meaning-searchers? Truth-seekers?

My guess is the philosophers
who did not call themselves that

didn't call themselves anything at all,
those wisdom lovers who loved their wisdom wild.

Soon It Will Be Spring

Soon it will be spring.
Do you know how strong spring is?
Do you know how strong it is to do what it does?
Of course you know.
You have seen spring before.
You have watched spring at work many times.
How it has to have the strength of a thousand winters
to wrestle winter to the ground,
then strangle winter with its bare hands,
then smother winter with whatever it finds at hand,
with snowdrops and crocus, to be certain,
then dig winter's grave deep in the ground,
so deep in the ground that winter will not stir again
until next winter.
And it has only its bare hands, mind you,
with which to do this.
Tell me, have you ever dug a hole with your bare hands?
I don't mean a hole for a tulip.
I mean a hole big enough to bury winter in?
This is how strong spring has to be.
And spring does this all alone.
It gets no help, not from us.
No, not from us who merely stand around, cheering.

Uncollecting

I'm giving my books to the library.
What else should I do with them?

Leave them on the shelves for my daughter to inherit?
What will she do with them?

Burn them?
Give them to the library?

Someday she will have to deal with empty shelves.
These shelves are big and heavy.

They will be burden enough for her.
No, I'm giving my books to the library.

The librarians are the book experts.
They will know which to keep, which to burn.

Emily At Two: A Photograph

Her nose rides
a rocking horse of smile.

Her dimples
are seeds of mouths.

Her hair is ragged,
a doll's hair

that a naughty
little girl has cut.

Her eyes
are retractable.

She has moved
them to the back of her head.

Swans

While the five swans swim,
many geese wait on the shore.
The swans swim. And swim.

March

All day a cold rain.
What has winter forgotten
coming back again?

A Pair Of Boxer Shorts Given Me As A Birthday Gift

When I go
to the bathroom

and pull my penis
through the fly to piss,

it's the fat king
of Hawaii coming out

of his hut
to join the women,

and when I jiggle
the drops off,

he's dancing with the one
he'll sleep with tonight.

Today Spring Leaves My Mind And Enters A Cloud

It is comfortable there is a cloud.
A cloud must therefore be the same
as the inside of my mind.

Today spring leaves a cloud and enters a tree.
It is comfortable there in a tree.
A tree must therefore be the same
as the inside of my mind.

Today spring leaves a tree and enters a stone.
It is comfortable there in a stone.
A stone must therefore be the same
as the inside of my mind.

I Am Looking Forward To Cremation

I am looking forward to not having a grave,
to being ash and then less,
to being dust and then less,
to being carbon, nitrogen, phosphorus,
to being numberless,
numberlessness.

Woodstock

Leaving the Golden Notebook book store,
I noticed an old beat sitting on a bench.

He was writing.
So I said, "Is that a poem?"

He looked up at me as though
I were about to steal his soul out

from under his scalp.
I suppose I was.

His Life At Home

Looking through the shed
for old things to throw away,
he found a 12 by 16 photograph
of his mother as a young woman
under glass in a wood frame
with a 3 by 5 snapshot of
his father as a young man stuck
in the lower left corner
of the frame on top of the glass.

The Most Dangerous People

The most dangerous people
are the geniuses.

Tell me, what moron
has ever been a serial-killer?

Tell me, what imbecile
has ever slaughtered millions?

Tell me, what half-wit
has ever starved tens of millions?

Fallen Barn

Like a house of cards,
this barn of cards
could not stand up
under one more ace of years.

Paterson

I cannot see it from the train.
So many buildings between us.
So much brick in the way.
Nor can I hear "the thunder
of the waters filling his dreams!"
But it is all right.
Anyway it is in my lap,
on the train, going with me,
the book with a picture of him
on the cover.
Laughing, laughing, laughing.

Daffodils

There are no daffodils.
The deer got them all.

I do not miss them.
There are so many other flowers.

Yet from time to time,
I take a long look at the fawns.

Are those white spots
a little yellow now?

Projection

Listen, since I don't like projects,
which is what your suggestion
sounds like to me, and a project
is anything I define that takes
an entire day or more to do,
I prefer the equivalent of a good
night's sleep, eight hours of
leaving the mind to its own
devices, the way the body devised it.

To A Student Who May Not Pass Writing

I too have a wish.
I wish I could make your wish come true.

I wish you will be the lawyer you wish to be.
I wish you will be the judge you wish to be afterward.

I wish it were as simple as that.
I wish it were twice as simple as that.

Wedding

The rehearsal lasted hours.
But the father of the bride
stood in the wrong place
anyway, and the flower girl
gave flowers to the wrong
people anyway, and the ring
bearer dropped the ring
anyway, and the minister
said the wrong name anyway,
and they got married anyway.

A Stone

Walking along the road, I paused
to kick a stone into the ditch.
Looking down at the stone, I said,
"Every day I am nearer to death, so
I envy anything that does not die,
even this stupid stone." Then the stone
no longer looked like the stone
I had kicked into the ditch but another one.

New York Movie By Edward Hopper

She's seen it a hundred times.
No wonder she's lost in thought.
But look at the screen which is
the silver mirror of her day dream.

The Golden Rule According To Emily

Undo others
before
others
undo you.

Reassurance

This morning, I found a
dead mouse at the bottom
of the driveway. "Don't
worry," said the crow
from a branch of the pear
tree. "Even a dead mouse
has its uses."

Bad Day At The Piano

Today you forgot
Chopin's address.

I heard your fingers
running around

the white avenues
and the black

side streets
looking for his house.

Claim To Fame

At the Linden Tree Inn
in Rockport,
Massachusetts,
I sat on
the same toilet seat
that Judy Collins
sat on.

Present

"What do you want for your birthday this year?" she asked.

"Let's just get something straight," he answered.

Dialogue

"You're so predictable," she said.
"You're a cartoon."

"What can I say?" he said.
"I'm out of my depth."

The Rain

is so cold,
it's almost ice,
while the ice
is so warm,
it's almost rain.

In Four Months

it will be April,
and my wild cherry
will bloom just as
it has bloomed
for forty Aprils.
Dear goddess
of my wild cherry,
I pray that I am
not here to see it
when it does not.

If It Weren't For

the dogwood
tree with its
white flowers
in the front yard,
I would have no
reason to look
up from the white
paper and out
the window at
that nothing out
there but green.

In The Middle Of The Lake

a pair of Canada geese.
How stately and serene they look
as they glide on the still water.
But this is only because
the swans are not here.

In Yosemite

I left an apple core
at the base of a pine.
I wasn't supposed to.
Neither was the raven
supposed to circle
and circle and circle
and come down to get it.
But I did, and he did.
An apple core at the core
of our twin temptations.
Such partners in crime,
weren't we, Brother Raven?

The Jonah Story

I do not like the Jonah story. The Jonah story is all obedience and disobedience, God calling on the wind to frighten the sailors, God calling on the whale to swallow up Jonah and spit him out again on dry land, God calling on the worm to desolate the vine. The Jonah story is all God calling. I do not like the way the Jonah story ends. The Jonah story ends without ending. It ends with God asking Jonah a question, but really asking one of those holy rhetorical questions that God is so fond of, and that is where Jonah is left hanging, on the question mark of God. And I do not like this because I want to know what happens to heroes at the end of stories. What happens to Jonah at the end of his story? What does Jonah do? Does he go home? Does he stay where he is on the east side of Nineveh where he prepares a field of gourd vines? Does he sleep twenty-four hours through? Does God leave Jonah alone? Does God leave Jonah alone, finally, oh finally, in the shade of the vine?

My Friend Jim Says

My friend Jim says
that you're not truly alive
until you kill.

He may be right.
He usually is right.
Someday I will list them all,

all the ways that he is right.
But for now I'm going to kill
the man who blinded my cat Ichabod.

Then I will be truly alive.
As Ichabod is truly alive.
As justice will,

for once in the world,
for a moment,
be truly alive.

I'm In Love With The Starbucks Mermaid

I'm in love with the Starbucks mermaid.
I'm in love with her Mona Lisa smile.

I'm in love with her eyes of inscrutable green.
Those big green eyes with no pupils.

I'm in love with her long hair of seaweed.
I'm in love with her two fish tails.

How they must wrap you twice around twice.
How they must embrace the very breath out of you.

I adore her crown, toy catamaran with a star for a sail.
Yes, I'm in love with this woman of Lear.

She's the woman who is woman above all adorable.
Yes, I'm in love with her, green and white maid de mer.

Yes, she's the one, she's the one I love.
I'm in love with this fair Melusine.

I'm in love with her.
I'm in love with the Queen of Caffeine.

Building Site

So intent on
watching

the ground-
breaking

for the new
skyscraper,

they did not
notice,

high above
their heads,

the clouds
clench

together
tighter.

Classroom

At the sound
of the siren

at least a block
away, why,

nevertheless,
does one turn,

knowing full well
one cannot possibly

see it, one's head
to the window?

Eden

We have lived without it
for so long, it must be clear

by now that we do not need it.
Maybe we need the memory

of it, or the mistake of it, the myth
of it, or maybe it is just the word

we need, that old beginning in which
we also find the end of need:

Eden, Eden, Eden.

Ten Dollars

I gave ten dollars today to a homeless woman. She was young, in her twenties. She had a dog and a cat. Nine weeks old she said. It was hot. The three of them were sitting on the sidewalk on Fourteenth Street. It was the sunny side of Fourteenth Street. Why she didn't sit on the shady side I don't know. Maybe the money was better on the sunny side. Maybe the passersby were more generous on the sunny side. I don't know. I didn't ask. It was very hot. I gave her ten. I do know this. The wrong people in this world have all the money. I wish I had lots of it, millions and millions. I would give it all to the homeless. I would give it to the girls and the dogs and the cats and the vets of Nam. But it's the wrong people who have the millions and millions. The poets should have all the money. The poets should have the millions and millions. The poets would know what to do with it. The poets wouldn't care what the homeless did with it. There would be no strings attached. Each would pursue happiness in his or her fashion. It would be just as Jefferson said. He, too, was among the wrong people with millions and millions. It's always the wrong people. I'm done with this poem tired of being a poem about a girl tired of being homeless in a country tired of being the richest country on an earth tired, oh, how tired, tired, tired of being the world. Walk down the sunny side of Fourteenth Street. You'll see what I mean.

Myopia

The window:
a sky composed of a single cloud
somewhere near the sun.

The desk lamp:
a sun diffused through fog
rising over a lake.

The green blotter on the desk:
a lake with fog rising.

My glasses on the desk beside the green blotter:
a bicycle rusting in the undergrowth
beside a lake.

My left hand:
three wild swans rising through
fog rising.

Forgetting The Book

Never mind.
I do not need it.
I remember the sound
well enough,
the broad, deep,
brooding wall of voice
in front of us,
like the slow close
of dark drapes before
the dark window,
before the dark rain,
before the dark night.

Apology To Mary Adoki

I forgot to dig up the bamboo
to give to the gardener's assistant.
I meant to do it before, but it rained.
I should have done it, but it is too late
now. I do not like not keeping my word.
It is small, for one to go back on one's
word, even if it is unintentional, even if
it is a small thing like digging up a clump
of bamboo for the gardener's assistant.
So I apologize to you, Mary Adoki, for not
digging up the bamboo I promised you,
and as penance I will suffer whatever evil
thoughts you think of me and the bony
scratching the bamboo branches make
against my window at night.

Orange Buds By Mail From Florida By Whitman

Do you know "Orange Buds by Mail from Florida"
by Whitman?
Do you know it?
If you do not know it, you should find it and know it.
You should go to your library
and find "Orange Buds by Mail from Florida"
or find it in your own dusty Whitman
on your own dusty shelf as I found it in my own
dusty Whitman on my own dusty shelf.
It is a poem that brags about America.
You will laugh when you read it.
You will laugh out loud when you read
how Whitman brags about America
in "Orange Buds by Mail from Florida,"
a good clean laugh, without sarcasm, without superiority,
without condescension, a good, clean, wholesome,
American, optimistic laugh.

Typo

How you laughed when
you read what the editor
of that magazine had done
to your poem, changing, in
the last line, "salvia," as
though it had been you who
had made the error, to "saliva."

October Rain

Hesitant before,
the leaves,
in the morning
downpour,
took leave
of the trees in
the thousands
and poured down
in their own rain.

The Dark Rabbi And The Rose Rabbi

The Dark Rabbi and the Rose Rabbi were not twins as the villagers believed. Before the Dark Rabbi was ordained, he wanted to be a philosopher. Before the Rose Rabbi was ordained, he wanted to be a composer of symphonies. The Dark Rabbi lived alone in a tower made of gray stone. The Rose Rabbi lived alone in a tower made of oaken boards. The Dark Rabbi spent his time studying the Talmud and looking for a wife who would look after him in his old age. The Rose Rabbi spent his time daydreaming about what his life could have been had his mother given him piano lessons. Although they were not twins, the Dark Rabbi and the Rose Rabbi alternated giving the Sabbath sermon and were often mistaken for one another. They died on the same day and were buried in the same grave. Both names were cut into the same stone.

Dunkin Donuts

I asked the college kid
at Dunkin Donuts what
he was studying at college.
"Psychology," he said.
"And why's that?" "So
I can know myself," he said.
"That's cool. A bachelor's in
psychology will certainly
help with that, but do you think,
honestly now, you can make
a living knowing yourself?"
"Sure," he said. "Why not?"
I gave him a $20 tip.

Wake

My neighbor dies the other day.
Today I go to his wake.
He was 77.

We weren't friends.
We were acquaintances.
We were neighbors.

We greeted one another on the road.
In the post office.
In the supermarket.

The word *wake* means to stay alert.
To watch.
To guard.

It comes from the Old English *wacian*
To be awake.
To keep watch.

I don't stay long.
I say to his widow, "I'm very sorry."
I hug her.

I talk to two neighbors about local politics.
About the price of gas.
About the new water mains.

About the weather.
About how he doesn't look 77.
About how unexpected it was.

Mostly about the weather.
I don't stay long.
I stay alert.

I watch.
I guard.
It is mostly about the weather.

It is cool but not cold.
It is mostly cloudy.
The sun comes out but doesn't stay long.

Him To The Sun

Him to the sun
is Adam's atom.

Subatomic subadamic.
This is him to the sun.

Utility

The utility pole
on the road
at the bottom
of the driveway
was once a tree
without utility.

A Brief Conversation

"What should I write?"
asked the young poet.

"Write what you feel,"
answered the old poet.

"I feel everything,"
said the young poet.

"Then write everything,"
said the old poet.

"But if I write everything now
when I'm young,

what will I write when I'm old?"
asked the young poet.

"You'll write everything
you remember of everything,"

answered the old poet
and waved the young poet away.

The End

The poems stop
not because
he loses his voice.

The poems stop
because
the poet goes deaf.

Tomorrow, Today, And Yesterday

Tomorrow I said,
This is where I am.

Today I said,
This is where I want to be.

Yesterday I said,
This was where I was supposed to be all along.

Acknowledgments

American Journal of Poetry: "Toy Poem"

Chronogram: "Building Site"; "Wake"

Foliate Oak Literary Magazine: "Eden"

Offcourse Literary Journal: "After the Movie"; "Dunkin Donuts"; "Gerald Stern"; "In the Waiting Room Waiting My Turn"; "Pythagoras Was the First Philosopher to Call Himself That"; "Uncollecting"

Under a Green Linden: "Soon It Will Be Spring"

One Sentence Poems: "Myopia"; "Question for Yahweh"; "Short Speech for Sisyphus"; "Someday the Last Poet in the World"

The Wax Paper: "Ten Dollars"